ViRUSES

Please visit our web site at: **www.garethstevens.com**
For a free color catalog describing Gareth Stevens Publishing's list of high-quality books and multimedia programs, call 1-800-542-2595 (USA) or 1-800-387-3178 (Canada). Gareth Stevens Publishing's fax: (414) 332-3567.

Library of Congress Cataloging-in-Publication Data

Contagious.
    Viruses.
       p. cm. — (Discovery Channel school science. Universes large and small)
    Summary: Discusses viruses, including their physical characteristics and some of the diseases they can cause.
    ISBN 0-8368-3375-9 (lib. bdg.)
    1. Viruses—Juvenile literature. 2. Virus diseases—Juvenile literature.
[1. Viruses. 2. Virus diseases.] I. Title. II. Series.
QR201.V55C665 2003
616'.0194—dc21
                              2003042497

This edition first published in 2004 by
Gareth Stevens Publishing
A World Almanac Education Group Company
330 West Olive Street, Suite 100
Milwaukee, WI 53212 USA

This U.S. edition copyright © 2004 by Gareth Stevens, Inc. First published in 1999 as *Contagious: The Virus Files* by Discovery Enterprises, LLC, Bethesda, Maryland. © 1999 by Discovery Communications, Inc.

Further resources for students and educators available at www.discoveryschool.com

Designed by Bill SMITH STUDIO
Creative Director: Ron Leighton
Design: Eric Hoffsten, Jay Jaffe, Brian Kobberger, Nick Stone, Sonia Gauba
Production Director: Paula Radding
Photo Editor: Justine Price
Art Buyer: Lillie Caporlingua
Print consulting by Debbie Honig, Active Concepts

Gareth Stevens Editor: Betsy Rasmussen
Gareth Stevens Art Director: Tammy Gruenewald
Technical Advisor: Sandya R. Govindaraju

Printed in the United States of America

1 2 3 4 5 6 7 8 9 07 06 05 04 03

Writers: Lynn Brunelle, Marc Gave

Photographs: Cover, flu virus, © NIBSC/Science Photo Library/Photo Researchers, Inc.; p. 3, Marine in biohazard suit, Corbis/Leif Skoogfors; p. 5, HIV, © NIBSC/ Science Photo Library/Photo Researchers, Inc.; p. 6, adenovirus particle, Philippe Plailly/Science Photo Library/Science Photo Library/Photo Researchers, Inc.; pp. 8-9, Brown Brothers (all); p. 10, wart virus, © Kwangshin Kim/Photo Researchers, Inc.; HIV, © NIBSC/Science Photo Library/Photo Researchers, Inc.; influenza virus, CNRI/Science Photo Library/Photo Researchers, Inc.; chicken pox virus, © Oliver Meckes/ Gelderblom/Photo Researchers, Inc.; yellow fever virus, © CDC/Science Source/Photo Researchers, Inc.; p. 11, rabies virus, © Chris Bjornberg/Photo Researchers, Inc.; hanta virus, © Scott Camazine/Photo Researchers, Inc.; p. 14, Ebola virus, © Science Source/Photo Researchers, Inc.;

bacteriophage, © Oliver Meckes/E.O.S./MPI-Tubingen/Photo Researchers, Inc.; p. 15, Hepatitis B virus, © Oliver Meckes/Ottawa/Photo Researchers, Inc.; HIV, © NIBSC/Science Photo Library/Photo Researchers, Inc.; influenza virus, CNRI/ Science Photo Library/Photo Researchers; p. 18, Corbis/Bettmann; p. 19, human forms, Corbis; innoculation shot, Brown Brothers; p. 20, mosquito, National Institutes of Health; p. 22, iron lung, Brown Brothers; polio virus, © Oliver Meckes/E.O.S./Gelderblom/Photo Researchers, Inc.; p. 23, Brown Brothers; p. 24, Marine in biohazard suit, Corbis/Leif Skoogfors; Ebola virus, © Science Source/Photo Researchers, Inc.; pp. 28-29, © Corel; p. 31, Ramses V, © Corel.

Illustrations: pp. 4-5, HIV and cell, Christopher Burke; pp. 12-13, sneeze invading cell, Bob Bruger; pp. 26-27, map, Joe LeMonnier.

VIRUSES

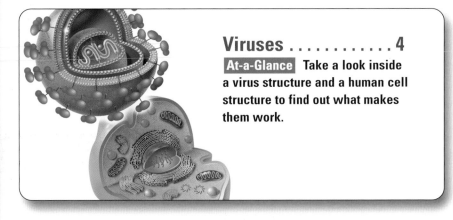

People get them. Animals get them. Plants get them. Viruses are everywhere. They are so small that you can only see them through an electron microscope, but viruses certainly can cause lots of trouble. While some are harmless—think about chicken pox after you've already had them—others are deadly.

In VIRUSES, Discovery Channel takes you inside a virus and then on a worldwide quest to find cures that will banish dreaded viral diseases. Viruses are as much a part of ordinary life as the common cold, but you'll discover, there's nothing "common" about these tiny troublemakers.

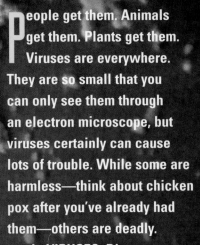

Dangerous Mission. See page 24

Final Project

3

Viruses

Nucleic Acids—Genetic information for the virus, in the form of RNA. These are the blueprints that are injected into a host cell for creating new viruses. In other viruses, the genetic material is DNA.

Feel healthy? Germ-free? Guess again. Invaders are slinking around your body right now, ready for a chance to take hold and take control of your cells. What will they do with your cells? They will use your cells to make copies of themselves. These tiny trespassers invade fungi, plants, animals, and even bacteria. No living thing is free of them. They are viruses, and they spell big trouble in tiny packages.

If you've ever had a cold, the flu, or chicken pox, then viruses have been *replicating* (making copies of themselves) like crazy inside your body. You can't see viruses, and they are invisible even under most microscopes. What are they? They are not cells because they have no nucleus or energy-making capabilities. And they can't reproduce by themselves. Viruses are parasites. Freeloaders. Moochers.

A single virus can either be called a virus or a virion. Different virions vary greatly in size, shape, and complexity, but they all share two basic structures: genetic material (DNA or RNA) and a coating. This drawing of a single HIV (Human Immunodeficiency Virus) getting ready to attack a human T4 helper cell shows those features. The drawing also shows additional features that allow us to identify this particular virus.

Virus Structure

Envelope—Lipid (fat) covering that surrounds the capsid in some viruses.

Capsid —Protein coat that protects the nucleic acid core.

Viral Proteins—These projections from the envelope allow the virion to recognize proteins in the host cell's membrane and attach itself to, and then enter, the host cell.

Protein Core —Housing for the genetic material.

Cell Structure

Ribosome (blue dots)—Protein factory. Ribosomes are the sites of protein synthesis.

Cytoplasm—Jellylike material within the cell membrane that contains mostly water and nutrients and is in constant motion. The cytoplasm surrounds organelles, which have specific functions.

Lysosome—Tiny, spherical organelle containing enzymes that break down large molecules so the cell can use them.

Nucleus—Core of the cell, which contains the genetic material DNA, often in the form of chromosomes.

Mitochondrion (*plural: Mitochondria*)—Respiration center that converts nutrients into energy for the cell.

Endoplasmic Reticulum—Membrane "highway" of folded sacs and tunnels through which materials travel through the cell. On its surface, proteins and new membranes are produced.

Cell Membrane—Outer boundary that separates the cell from other cells and its environment. The membrane allows certain molecules to pass through and keeps others out.

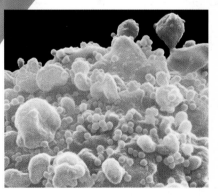

Above: Shows a more accurate scale of viruses (green) to cell.

Get a Life

Q: You're a *Rhinovirus,* aren't you? Also known as the common cold?

A: I much prefer the first name. So much more dignified. So much more interesting. So much less . . . common. Besides, if I'm so common, why is there no cure for me?

Q: I guess you have a point. Actually, you have lots of points. Why DO you have all those pointy parts sticking out?

A: They're called receptors, and they're very handy. They allow me to attach myself to your cells.

Q: Ouch. Why would you want to do that?

A: Simple. So that I can pierce the cell membrane and get inside the cell.

Q: Ouch—and yuck!

A: Oh, don't be such a baby. It's just what viruses do. It's what we HAVE to do. In some viruses, the genetic material is DNA. Mine is RNA. But we all do the same thing with it: get into a cell.

Q: What do you mean, you HAVE to do it?

A: It's the only way we can have a life. See, viruses aren't alive. We can't grow and reproduce on our own. We're not like a human cell, which reproduces by dividing into two cells. We need a host cell to . . . shall we say, visit. A place to hang out and make copies of ourselves.

Q: You mean a place to invade. Attack. Mooch off. You . . . you . . . you parasite!

A: It's nothing personal. Besides, we can't help it. And I don't attach myself to all your cells. Only certain ones—like the ones in your nose and throat. That's how I got my name, in fact. Rhino means "nose" in Greek. You breathe me in through your nose, and then I do my pierce-squirt-copy thing.

Q: Charming. But do all viruses attack only certain types of cells?

A: Yep. We all have different specialties. We all have different shapes, too. Some viruses are shaped like me. Some are shaped like crystals. Some look like little spaceships. It's too bad more people can't see us to appreciate what a truly handsome bunch we are. We get around in different ways, too. Some of us travel through the air, like me. Some travel in water. Some make their way into food. And others are in blood or other stuff in your body.

Q: Besides being freeloaders, don't viruses have anything else in—common?

A: Would you stop saying that? But yes, we do have similarities. We all have several layers. Our envelope is the outside layer, made of fatty stuff. The envelope surrounds our capsid, or our protein shell. And our DNA or RNA is at the center.

Q: The stuff you shoot inside MY cells!

A: Right. We inject genetic material and the cell becomes our slave—a virus factory—cranking out copies of us until it gets full to bursting.

Q: How long does that take?

A: Depends on the kind of virus. Viruses that use a process called the lytic cycle start copying right away. After a day or two, the host cell is so full of copies it bursts like a balloon. But viruses called temperate viruses enter a host cell and

stick around for a while without doing any harm. Then something happens—like a burst of certain chemicals or radiation —and bam, the viruses do what they do best. Copy, copy, copy.

Q: That's so unfair! Isn't there anything humans can do?

A: Well, your body isn't exactly defenseless. It has a great line of defense called the immune system. It's like a security force of killer cells that patrol the body looking for intruders. They get help from proteins called antibodies, which recognize viruses when they invade. The antibodies usually stick to the viruses and stop them, so the killer cells can come in and gobble them up.

Q: What do you mean, usually?

A: The antibodies don't always recognize the viruses. Sometimes the viruses can sneak right in.

Q: Uh-oh. But that's where antibiotics come in, right? They can fight back.

A: Afraid not. Antibiotics are for fighting bacteria, not viruses. But you're on the right track. Vaccines can help. A vaccine is a small amount of a weakened or inactive virus that is introduced into your immune system. Your body then makes antibodies to fight the disease, and it is quickly eliminated. If that virus ever comes along, the antibodies will immediately recognize the intruder and kill i t before it has a chance to take over.

Q: So why isn't there a vaccine for the common cold?

A: Well, viruses can mutate, or change their chemistry. That makes it difficult to develop a vaccine. Besides, there are lots of viruses for which there are currently no vaccines. HIV is one. And the *Rhinovirus*—my decidedly uncommon self—is another. But I've got to be going now. I have places to . . . visit.

Q: Say, is that a tickle I feel in my throat?

Activity

SHOT IN THE ARM Why do some people get a flu shot every year? How does this relate to vaccines and viruses? Use reference books or the Internet to research this topic. Discuss the pros and cons of annual flu shots.

Pox and the People

Viruses have been around longer than people, infecting organisms and using the organism's cells as factories to produce copies of themselves so they can survive. It was only a matter of time before people started to use viruses for their own advantages and disadvantage.

ACCIDENTAL ASSASSINS

Mexico, 1519

When Hernando Cortès invaded Mexico, he had only a small army. There was no way he could conquer the huge Aztec Empire. But conquer it he did with the help of a tiny warrior—the smallpox virus. Cortès didn't know his army had brought the virus with them; in fact, he didn't even know what a virus was. But the Aztecs had no immunity to smallpox, and many of them that came into contact with the virus suffered the disease. Four million people died as a result of this accidental viral warfare.

Viruses as Healers?

Viruses are known to cause diseases, but they can also be used to help cure diseases. Because viruses are experts at injecting genetic information into a cell and harnessing that cell to create new viruses, scientists have been working on ways to manipulate the kind of information a virus can inject into a cell. To have viruses inject other kinds of information, in the form of DNA, into cells is called gene therapy. This kind of therapy might be able to stop cancer and AIDS and cure genetic disorders such as cystic fibrosis.

Massachusetts, 1634

Not so accidental was the white settlers' use of the smallpox virus to get rid of the local Native American population in the colonies. One notable example was Lord Jeffrey Amherst's distribution to the Indians of blankets infested with the smallpox virus. After the distribution, the Indians fell prey to the deadly disease. This allowed the settlers to expand their territory.

Turkish Delight

Lady Mary Wortley Montagu, wife of the British Ambassador to Turkey, witnessed primitive vaccinations. In a letter to her friend Sarah Chiswell, she writes:

I am going to tell you a thing that will make you wish yourself here. The small-pox, so fatal, and so general amongst us, is here entirely harmless, by the invention of ingrafting, which is the term they give it. There is a set of old women, who make it their business to perform the operation, every autumn in the month of September, when the great heat is abated.

People send to one another to know if any of their family has a mind to have the small-pox; they make parties for this purpose, and when they are met, the old woman comes with a nut-shell full of the matter of the best sort of small-pox, and asks what vein you please to have opened.

She immediately rips what you offer her with a large needle (which gives you no more pain than a common scratch) and puts into the vein, as much matter as can lie upon the head of her needle, and after that binds up their little wound with a hollow bit of shell; and in this manner opens up four or five veins... .

The children or young patients play together all the rest of the day, and are in perfect health to the eighth. Then the fever begins to seize them, and they keep their beds two days, very seldom three. There is no example of anyone that died in it: and you may believe I am well satisfied of the safety of this experiment, since I intend to try it on my dear little son. I am patriot enough to take pains to bring this useful invention into fashion in England. . . .

When Lady Mary returned to England, doctors refused to have anything to do with the procedure. The Prince of Wales allowed her to have an experiment conducted in a prison, promising that volunteers for inoculations would be pardoned—if they survived. They did, and King George I was so delighted that he had his grandchildren inoculated. But the practice was deemed dangerous and abandoned until the end of the century, when a country doctor named Edward Jenner took matters into his own hands. (see p. 18)

Beauty and the Virus

You know it's spring when you have a vase of beautiful tulips on the table. Pinks, yellows, and stripes. What does this have to do with viruses? Well, those stripes and bright color streaks are caused by viruses. Today, this virus is cultivated, but hundreds of years ago, it all began with an infection. In Holland in the 1600s, these infected tulips were highly prized. Their color combinations and sassy streaks were stunningly beautiful. People traded bulbs like jewels. Farmers offered their daughters' hands in marriage and even sold their farms for the thrill of owning one infected bulb. That's one veritably valuable virus!

Activity

MAKE YOUR OWN SCRAPBOOK Viruses make the headlines all the time. Keep track of viral action by gathering interesting articles about viruses and diseases. Look for images in magazines, newspapers, and on the Internet. Look at advertisements. How do people use diseases to sell? How are viruses both harmful and helpful? Over time, gather all the articles and photographs that relate to viruses and diseases and the effects that viruses have on people and the environment. Write down notes and make illustrations to keep in your scrapbook. How do viruses affect you? Your family? Your school? The country? The world?

Warts and All

Viruses have been plaguing living things since the dawn of life. They float around, waiting for a chance to infect a host cell and multiply inside it. Different viruses are responsible for different ailments. Some are limited in what organisms they can attack. Some can sicken just one species, but others can sicken many different species. Viruses don't ask if they can visit, and once they're inside, many outstay their welcome. It's awfully tough being a gracious host to a virus.

Warts

Warts pop up in the most embarrassing places, such as your hands, where you can't hide them. They're not caused by kissing frogs or by evil spells. Tiny viruses replicate inside your skin cells, creating the unsightly and sometimes painful warts.

AIDS

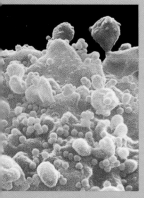

AIDS probably originated in monkeys. It strikes people the world over. It is caused by HIV (Human Immunodeficiency Virus), which attacks the body's own defense system. HIV gets inside the white blood cells—the body's disease-fighting cells—and replicates. As the body's defenses weaken, the body becomes vulnerable to other diseases, such as pneumonia.

Cold and flu

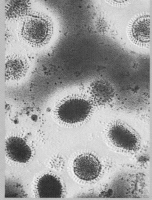

Cold and flu are sometimes mistaken for one another. There are about three hundred different cold viruses. They go straight to the cells in the lining of your nose, giving you the sniffles and perhaps a sore throat. Fever, cough, and body aches mean you may have the flu. The lungs, too warm for a cold virus, are the perfect climate for the flu.

Smallpox

Smallpox has probably killed up to 100 million people in its history and left 200 million blind and scarred. Officially wiped out in 1980, this viral disease produces pimplelike pustules on the skin. In one of the great success stories in the history of diseases, the smallpox virus has been eliminated from the human population, the result of a successful World Eradication Program. Some of this virus remains in laboratory use, and much debate surrounds its future.

Chicken pox

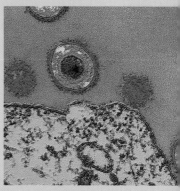

Chicken pox comes with nasty-little-itchy-bumps, but once you've had them, you never get them again. The body fights off the virus and remembers it. If the virus ever comes in contact with your body again, it's blasted out before it can get a foothold.

Yellow fever

Yellow fever got its name because it attacks the liver, giving its victim jaundice, which causes a yellow appearance. This disease is passed along by mosquitoes. When a mosquito sucks the blood of an infected person, it sucks in viruses along with blood. When it bites its next victim, it passes those viruses into the bloodstream. Nowadays, people can protect themselves from some viruses with a vaccine.

Small Compared to What?

Viruses are so small that they are measured in nanometers (nm). One nanometer is one-billionth of a meter—that's 1/1,000,000,000! But within the virus community, size varies quite a bit. Here are sizes and other information about ten familiar culprits that were or are still widespread among humans:

Disease	Size (nm)	How transmitted	Symptoms and results
Chicken pox	150–200	Air currents	Fever, rash
HIV	110	Sexual contact; contaminated blood, syringes, and needles	Failure of immune system; leads to AIDS
Infectious hepatitis	20–30	Contaminated food or water	Fever, chills, joint aches, nausea, jaundice
Influenza (flu)	80–120	Air currents	Fever, nose and throat congestion, rash
Mononucleosis	150–200	Air currents	Swollen salivary glands
Mumps	100	Contaminated food or water	Rash, swollen glands
Poliomyelitis (polio)	20	Air currents	Headache, stiff neck, paralysis
Smallpox	250	Air currents	Fever, skin pustules; was often fatal
Yellow fever	22	Mosquitoes	Fever, aches, nausea, liver-cell destruction; can be fatal

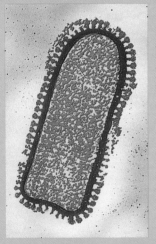

Rabies is passed along when dogs, raccoons, and other infected mammals bite another mammal. Rabies targets the nervous system. Because it doesn't travel in the blood, immune systems aren't involved. Once the virus reaches the brain, there is nothing to be done. Protect yourself by vaccinating your pets and by avoiding any weird-acting or sick animal. If you do get bitten, wash the wound IMMEDIATELY and call for help. Rabies can be stopped if caught early enough.

Hanta Virus gets passed to humans through rodents, usually deer mice. People inhale contaminated dust from mouse droppings or nests, and they come down with flu-like symptoms. This quickly leads to acute congestion in the lungs. Over 50 percent of hanta virus cases have been fatal, and there is no effective treatment yet available.

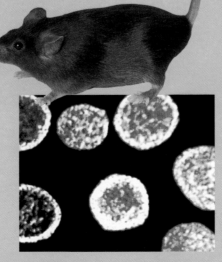

Even Plants Get Viruses

Tobacco mosaic virus was the first viral plant disease discovered. This virus withers healthy tobacco leaves, leaving the plant weakened and sometimes unable to produce food from the Sun.

Even Germs Get Germs

Bacteriophage means "bacteria-eater" in Greek. This is a virus that looks like a landing pod. With its six legs, the bacteriophage attaches to the surface of a bacteria much larger than itself. Most phages have tails, the tips of which have the ability to bind to specific molecules on the surface of their target bacteria. The viral DNA is then injected through the tail into the host cell, where it directs the production of offspring phages—sometimes over one hundred in half an hour. An infected bacterium creates so many copies of the bacteriophage that the cell bursts. Infection means death for a single-celled bacterium.

Ah-choo!

Opportunity Doesn't Always Knock

You're a virus. You're so small that you're invisible to humans. That's what makes you so powerful. You're out there and you get around. Depending on what kind of virus you are, you can travel from one place to another by way of an animal bite, a kiss, a cut, or a sneeze. Right now, you happen to be in a sneeze.

The Sneeze

Ah-choo! Until that dreaded sound, you were resting comfortably in Lisa's nose. Well, maybe you knew something was coming. You felt a little rumbling—the tickle at the back of Lisa's throat. Then there was a high wind—a deep breath she took.

But that sneeze really causes problems for you. As her nose and mouth let loose with billions of tiny droplets of spit and mucus, you go charging through the air. You don't have any way to stop it, but you know what you need to do. You need to find a new host that you can use and abuse.

The Spread

As luck would have it, Lisa sneezed while passing Joe in the hallway.

"Sorry!" she calls.

But it's too late. You're in. Inside one of Joe's nostrils, that is. You sail past thousands of your buddies who have gotten bogged down by the mucus and cilia (little hairs). They might eventually get swept toward Joe's throat, but you're lucky. You landed squarely at the back of Joe's throat.

The Infection

You go into action, knowing just what to do. You get your "hooks" to line up neatly with projections from a cell in Joe's throat. Wham!—the two of you stick together. You send out a tiny piercer to break into the cell, like a burglar breaking into a safe. You did it! Now, you immediately shove all your genetic material into the cell.

The Replication
Most viruses have DNA as their genetic material. But you're not like most viruses. You have RNA. Now the RNA directs the cell to create copies of you instead of going about its usual cellular business.

The Bursting of the Host Cell
These copies aren't the best guests because they are lots of copies of you. Bye-bye cell, hello viruses. It's breakout time, right through the cell membrane. Now more cells can be taken over and an army of viruses that all look like you can be created.

The Sickness
Later that day, after "soldier" viruses have made countless replications, Joe has the beginnings of a sore throat, and his nose is running like a faucet. He doesn't feel so good. That's no surprise to you—viruses have taken over. But wait! Joe's body is rallying, and now there's going to be an all-out war. Oceans of mucus flow from his nose trying to sweep away the invaders, and white blood cells flood the scene, trying to help eliminate the infected cells. In a matter of time, your clones are surrounded. It looks like curtains. But . . .

The Sneeze, Part II
There's a tickle in Joe's throat and a deep breath in and ah . . . ah . . . ah-CHOO! Who's next?

Activity

SEE HOW THEY SPREAD Try to get your entire school to participate in this. Someone in your class has to tell two other kids something and have those kids pass it on to two other kids—and so on. It should be a simple statement, and it should be written on a piece of paper in the presence of the teller to make sure it is accurate. At the end of the day, count up how many kids got the message. That will give you some idea about how a virus can invade one cell and wind up spreading so quickly.

READY FOR YOUR CLOSE-UP

TAKE A LOOK AT THESE TINY TERRORS:

Colorized images of viruses can give us a sense of what viruses look like. Though viruses can cause problems for us, their structures are really quite stunning.

Viruses are tiny. They're SMALL, SMALL, SMALL!! Not only can't you see them with just your eyes, you can't see them under an average microscope, either. They're just too small. To see viruses, you need to look through an electron microscope—a microscope that can peer at the smaller than small. The electron microscope changed the course of history. It produces a highly magnified image of a tiny object using an accelerated electron beam, held within a vacuum to illuminate the object, and electro-magnetic fields, to magnify and focus the image. First developed in Germany about 1932, the electron microscope allows the images it produces to be photographed or to be shown on a fluorescent screen.

BACTERIOPHAGE attacking a bacterium. This virus's secret weapon is in the genetic material it injects through the tip of its tail.

EBOLA VIRUS These rod-shaped viruses are extremely deadly.

14

HEPATITIS B VIRUS
This virus causes an inflamed liver, which can lead to the organ's deterioration.

FLU VIRUS
Influenza, or flu, is a lower respiratory infection that inflames and harms the larynx, trachea, and bronchi.

Activity

MAKE A MODEL OF A BACTERIOPHAGE

What you need:
- toothpicks
- plastic wrap
- string
- pipe cleaners
- hot glue gun (get an adult to help out with this because the glue is HOT!)

What you do:
Have a look at the picture of a bacteriophage. You may need other references as well. This virus is made up of three parts—*the capsid* (which encloses the genetic material), the *sheath*, and the *tail fibers*. Use the materials listed above to create your own bacteriophage. Make sure the parts are in relative size to each other and label them. How would you change things to make a different kind of virus?

HIV
By attacking and killing immune system cells, HIV (green) destroys the body's ability to fight infections and some kinds of cancers.

The DEADLIEST MONTH

Across the United States, October 1918

The United States has been fighting against the Central Powers in World War I for more than a year, and it looks like the end is in sight. But this month is the deadliest month in the nation's history, with 195,000 American fatalities. Most of them are not soldiers killed in European battles, however. They are victims in their own beds, stalked by an unseen killer, influenza, or the flu. Where did the flu come from, and why could nothing be done about it before it infected so many people? Let's go back a few months to find out.

Fort Riley, KS, March 11, 1918

Just before breakfast, company cook Albert Gitchell reports to the camp doctor with a "bad cold." By noon, more than one hundred men are sick with similar complaints. Two days earlier, a dust storm, combined with burning manure from thousands of army horses and mules, had created an eerie haze above the fort.

On the move, Spring 1918

At Fort Riley, forty-eight soldiers die. The cause of death is listed as pneumonia. Evidence that an epidemic is in the making comes from there and other military bases and prisons, which can monitor their residents more closely than civilian governments. But before anything can be done, 84,000 American soldiers ship out to Europe in March, followed by 118,000 in April. A number of them are carrying what would eventually be identified as the flu virus. Six soldiers die on one ship crossing the Atlantic Ocean.

Around the world, May–July

The mysterious disease has established itself in Europe, and the loss of soldiers on both sides of the battle have caused war plans to be changed. By early summer, cases are reported in Russia, North Africa, India, China, Japan, the Philippines, and New Zealand. Unknown to anyone, the flu mutates, or changes—something viruses do. By the time it returns to the United States, it is a ruthless killer. People still don't even realize the disease is the flu, because it is unlike any they have ever seen.

Boston, MA, Late August–September, 1918

Within two weeks of its first appearance, 2,000 navy men at a barracks known as the Receiving Ship have become sick. Chelsea Naval Hospital, across the bay, is overflowing with patients. On examination of the dead, the medical staff is shocked by what they find: bloody, foamy liquid that has drowned the lungs. Soon after, three civilians in nearby Quincy drop dead. A "Win the War for Freedom" parade through the streets of Boston does much to spread the flu to the general population. That's because it travels from person to person every time someone breathes out and someone else breathes in. At the end of the month, 1,000 people are dead in Boston, and the flu is spreading along the eastern seaboard, threatening the country—and the whole world.

The doctors don't know any more about the flu than was known about the Black Death in fourteenth-century Italy. Little is known about viruses, because the electron microscope that will allow viruses to be seen hasn't been invented yet.

Nationwide, October, 1918

- People can be healthy in the morning and dead by evening.
- Schools, theaters, churches—any place people congregate in great numbers—are closed.
- In some cities, people are ordered to wear masks in public. But the masks don't help because the viruses are too small to be kept out.
- People live in deadly fear because science is powerless to come up with a cure.
- Some try their own home remedies: camphor balls in little sacks around the neck, turpentine and kerosene on sugar, prayer.
- Quarantines of entire towns are set up.
- There are rumors that the Germans have started the epidemic.
- A children's playground rhyme:
  I had a little bird
  Its name was Enza
  I opened up the window
  And in flew Enza.

Camp Devens, MA, September 29, 1918

The following is an excerpt from a letter sent by an army doctor to a friend and colleague.

My dear Burt,
It is more than likely that you would be interested in the news of this place, for there is a possibility that you will be assigned here for duty, so having a minute between rounds, I will try to tell you a little about the situation here as I have seen it in the last week. . . .
Camp Devens is near Boston, and has about 50,000 men, or did have before this epidemic broke loose. It also has the base hospital for the Division of the Northeast. This epidemic started about four weeks ago, and has developed so rapidly that the camp is demoralized and all ordinary work is held up till it has passed. Mass assemblages of soldiers [are] taboo. These men start with what appears to be an attack of la grippe or influenza, and when brought to the hospital they very rapidly develop the most vicious type of pneumonia that has ever been seen. Two hours after admission they have the mahogany spots over the cheek bones, and a few hours later you can begin to see the cyanosis [blueness] extending from their ears and spreading all over the face. . . . It is only a matter of a few hours then until death comes, and it is simply a struggle for air until they suffocate.

November, 1918

Almost as rapidly as the flu came on, it starts to disappear. On November 11, the war ends. People celebrate in San Francisco, parading through the streets, wearing masks. On November 21, residents are allowed to remove their masks.

December, 1918

Five thousand new cases of flu are reported in San Francisco. Apparently, the epidemic isn't quite over.

Activity

WHO HAS THE RIGHT? During the flu epidemic of 1918, local governments took measures to try to keep the epidemic from spreading. Public places were closed, whole towns were quarantined, and people were forced to wear masks. Do you think the government has the right to impose such regulations at the sacrifice of individual rights? Have your teacher help you set up two three-person teams to debate this issue. Do research to prepare. Students need not take the position that they personally believe in to make the debate effective.

Little Things Count

H umans have probably always suffered from diseases caused by viruses. But people didn't know what viruses were until recently. Before that, causes for viral diseases were attributed to gods, spirits, the evil eye, and other mysterious forces.

When a more scientific approach was taken, investigators thought they might find the presence of bacteria in tissue samples of sick people. They were dumbfounded when they didn't see any. Scientists didn't know about viruses because they couldn't see them —viruses are too small. Much smaller than bacteria. So pioneers in the field of virology had to work more or less in the dark. They knew what worked, but not how or why.

England, 1796	France, 1885	Holland, 1900	Cuba, 1901	World War I, 1914–1918

England, 1796

Country doctor Edward Jenner notes that milkmaids who are exposed to cowpox become mildly ill, but they do not get smallpox, an often fatal disease. Inspired by a folk remedy, he takes pus from the cowpox sores of Sarah Nelmes and vaccinates eight-year-old James Phipps with it. James does not become sick. Despite the success of this experiment, no one knows what causes smallpox.

France, 1885

Louis Pasteur builds on Jenner's success and develops a vaccine against rabies, saving the life of nine-year-old Joseph Meister. Pasteur suspects that the cause of rabies is too small to be seen with the microscopes of the day—and he's right.

Holland, 1900

Botanist Martinus Willem Biejerinck names the invisible pathogens *viruses*, from the Latin word for poison.

Cuba, 1901

American military physician Walter Reed proves that yellow fever is caused by a virus transmitted by the bite of the female *Aedes aegypti* mosquito. In 1886, Carlos Finlay, a physician in Cuba, had run experiments to prove the same thing, but his ideas had been ignored by the scientific community.

France, 1917

Félix d'Herelle discovers bacteriophages and suggests they are kinds of viruses.

Worldwide, 1918

Flu epidemic sweeps many countries, leaving 30 million people dead. It is unlike any other flu reported. Health officials are slow to identify it and are at a loss as to how to treat it.

1935–1940	United States, 1940s–early 1950s	United States, 1964	1960s–1970s	United States, 1983–1990s

Many kinds of viruses are finally visible through the recently invented electron microscope. American biochemist Wendell Stanley, working with the tobacco mosaic virus, proves that viruses contain protein.

Two English biochemists discover that viruses also contain nucleic acids.

The polio virus strikes in epidemic proportions, causing widespread disability and panic. It is unclear how polio is spread. Franklin D. Roosevelt, president of the United States from 1933 to 1945, lost the use of his legs when stricken by polio in 1921.

In 1954, research physician Jonas Salk, working at the University of Pittsburgh (PA), develops the first vaccine effective against polio.

Molecular biologist Howard Temin proposes that some viruses use RNA to get the host cell to produce DNA, which instructs the host to produce new viruses. It takes ten years before his idea is accepted, when the first actual "retroviruses" are discovered.

The World Health Organization mounts a program to vaccinate people worldwide to try to eliminate smallpox. The disease is officially declared eliminated on May 8, 1980.

Researchers Richard Mulligan and David Baltimore bring their field into a new era by developing ways to use viruses to help, not harm, humans. They use genetically engineered DNA introduced into cells to treat genetic disorders. It's called "gene therapy."

Activity

TO KILL A VIRUS Smallpox was declared eliminated worldwide in 1980. But two collections of the virus remain frozen in vials, under heavy security. One is in Atlanta, Georgia, at the Center for Disease Control, and the other is in Moscow, Russia. Should these viruses be destroyed? Research the reasons for and against, and set up a debate between members of your class. You need not hold the opinion of the side you argue for the debate to be effective.

JUST ONE BITE

Cuba, 1898

During the Spanish-American War, more than 5,000 soldiers died of disease—over four times as many as died in combat. Of the many diseases that swept through the American camps, yellow fever was the most feared. It killed between 8 and 9 of every 10 people who got it. The disease had a long and terrible history stretching back to before Columbus's expedition to the Americas. Between 1596 and 1900, more than 90 epidemics struck parts of what is now the United States.

BLACK VOMIT

For those fortunate not to know yellow fever firsthand, the following is a typical course of the disease: First, you experience chills and a headache. Severe pains in the back, arms, and legs follow, accompanied by high fever and vomiting. The fever stage might last hours, days, or weeks. Jaundice, from which yellow fever derives its name, might then appear. Then comes the so-called stage of calm, when the severity of your symptoms subsides and the fever drops. If yours is a less serious case, this stage might indicate recovery. But it is more likely that this stage is followed by a return of the fever, accompanied by jaundice produced by the destruction of the liver, and the projectile vomiting of black blood caused by internal bleeding. This last aspect is the source of the other popular name of the disease, "the black vomit."

Cuba, May 1900

CONTROLLING A KILLER

Florida, U.S.

Cuba

Major Walter Reed, a military physician, was appointed president of a team of army research scientists to study the cause and spread of yellow fever in Cuba.

In 1881, Dr. Carlos Juan Finlay had specified the *Aedes aegypti* mosquito as the vector—an organism that transmits a pathogen—for the disease. But no one had paid much attention. Reed approached Finlay, who was pleased to have someone listen to him. On August 1, 1900, the team came to a decision. It would repeat Finlay's discredited experiment of having mosquitoes bite yellow fever patients and then healthy persons.

Walter Reed saw his first case of yellow fever the day he arrived at Las Animas Hospital outside Havana, Cuba. Dr. James Carroll was in bed with it, deliberately infected with one of the team's "experimental mosquitoes." In the autopsies of victims the team conducted in the next month or so, the four investigators first tried to find *Salmonella icteroides*, a bacterium that had been suggested as the cause of yellow fever. Reed concluded correctly that the bacterium was not the cause.

"As the idea that Carroll's fever must have been caused by the mosquito that was applied to him four days before became fixed upon our minds," wrote another team member, "we decided to test it upon the first non-immune person who should offer himself to be bitten.

"Within 15 minutes of the decision a soldier came by the laboratory door, and after gazing for a minute or two at the insects, he said:

'You still fooling around with mosquitoes, Doctor?'

'Yes, will you take a bite?'

'Sure, I ain't scared of 'em,' said the man, William H. Dean of Troop B, Seventh Cavalry."

The soldier came down with yellow fever. He was their first purely experimental case. Fortunately, he recovered from his bite. Sadly, in September, a team member came down with yellow fever from a stray mosquito and never recovered. His case was particularly horrific, ending in wild delirium and black vomit. Reed pondered the next step. Data he had gathered showed there was always a lag, averaging twelve days between the first appearance and the second stage of yellow fever. Reed had found the same time break in mosquito transmission of malaria. This similarity indicated mosquitoes as possible culprits in yellow fever transmission as well.

More experiments were conducted. In the first, the team exposed American volunteers to soiled and bloody clothing, towels, and bedding of yellow fever patients, which were thought to be the cause of infection. When they did not catch the fever, it proved that the disease could no be passed from this sort of contact. In the second, 11 of 13 volunteers (mostly Spanish immigrants who were paid $100 in gold) acquired yellow fever from the bites of infected mosquitoes.

The cause was determined to be something that was passed from one person's blood to another, but what? Efforts to find the yellow fever "germ" under the microscope failed. (It would take the invention of the electron microscope before scientists could view viruses.) After continued experimentation with filtered serum injected into patients, Reed and Carroll concluded that they were dealing with a microorganism so small that it could not be trapped by the finest filter, much as Pasteur had proposed that a tiny agent was the cause of rabies.

It was up to Havana health officers to deal the final blow. "If it is the mosquito," the sanitarian

Major William Gorgas told Reed, "I am going to get rid of the mosquito." Infected patients were put in isolation during their infected periods, and the rooms were fumigated afterward. Health officials also set about the task of killing adult mosquitoes and their larvae. Thus began the gigantic task of attacking the breeding places of mosquitoes. Every water container in the city would have to be addressed. Citizens began assuring inspectors: *"No hay mosquitos aquí, señor."* (We have no mosquitoes here, sir.)

For 140 years—from 1762 to 1901—Havana had not seen a day without a report of yellow fever. Gorgas launched his campaign in March, and by the following October, no more yellow fever was being reported.

Afterword: Progress Report on Yellow Fever

Yellow fever still occurs, especially in Central America, the northern half of South America, and Central Africa. Vaccination is the only sure prevention. Use of mosquito repellents, full body clothing, and screened housing will decrease exposure risk. Mosquito control has also decreased the risk. Risks remain, however, because the mosquito has increasing resistance to insecticides. There is no specific treatment for yellow fever.

Activity

PANAMA FEVER Walter Reed's work with yellow fever allowed the United States to succeed in building a canal across the isthmus of Panama, beginning in 1904, which joined the Atlantic and the Pacific Oceans. The construction team succeeded where a French group had failed some 20 years before—when work had to be halted due to yellow fever.

Now that you're acquainted with Reed and his work, you might enjoy visiting a web site called "The Panama Puzzle" at http://www-micro.msb.le.ac.uk/Tutorials/Panama/Panama.html. Take the quiz and see how you do.

Cracking the Crippling Killer

By the end of the summer of 1916, 27,000 people had been struck with a disease that would cripple them, and more than 10,000 had died. Each year after that, there was an epidemic of polio somewhere in the United States.

Polio struck people regardless of age, health, or income. Even Franklin Delano Roosevelt was struck, years before he became president of the United States. People who had lost the use of their diaphragm were encased in a machine called an iron lung (below left), which breathed for them.

People thought this disease spread through lakes and ponds, so they abandoned swimming. Now we know that the tiny virus enters into the body by the mouth, infecting the stomach cells and the intestines. If not conquered at this point, the virus moves to the nervous system, causing paralysis. Depending on the severity, the paralysis may go away, but in many cases, it can last a lifetime.

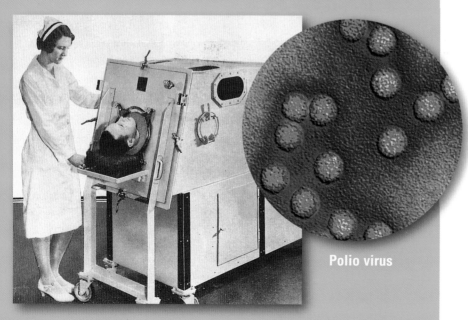

Polio virus

MAN OF THE HOUR

Jonas Salk became famous overnight after he announced that he had developed a vaccine against polio. But his accomplishments didn't happen overnight.

In the mid-1930s, Salk was in his second year of medical school when he had a vision of what he might accomplish. As Salk himself told the story: "We were told in one lecture that it was possible to immunize against diphtheria and tetanus by the use of chemically treated toxins, or toxoids. And the following lecture, we were told that for immunization against a virus disease, you have to experience the infection, and that you could not induce immunity with the so-called "killed" or inactivated chemically treated virus preparation. Well . . . what struck me was that both statements couldn't be true. And I asked why this was so, and the answer that was given was in a sense, 'Because.' There was no satisfactory answer. Perhaps it had been tried and not succeeded. I think that, in fact, was true."

Two years later, in his last year in medical school, Salk had the opportunity to test whether he could destroy a virus with chemicals and still immunize with it so that the body recognizes the real thing when it comes along. The influenza virus had just been

Dr. Jonas Salk's polio vaccine had its first widespread use in 1955.

discovered and he used it. The flu epidemic of 1918 had killed hundreds of thousands of Americans, and Salk worked out ways to make the virus safe for vaccines. This work laid the ground for his work on the polio vaccine.

Salk took polio viruses and "killed" them with formaldehyde. Then the killed viruses would be made into a vaccine and injected into a person. Their body would learn to recognize polio and make antibodies that would kill the virus in the bloodstream. Then if the real virus showed up, the antibodies would kill them before they had a chance to take over. That vaccinated person would be protected.

After Salk made his vaccine, he had to test it on people before he knew it would work. In an act of confidence, he first vaccinated himself and his family. Then he went on to run trials on thousands of kids and adults. It worked. People didn't get sick even when exposed to the live virus. Jonas Salk had found his answer. And as a result of his work, polio is something you may never have to worry about getting.

Jonas Salk never stopped questioning when he saw a contradiction. He didn't accept pat assertions if there was a reason to think otherwise. After the polio vaccine was distributed worldwide, he might have rested on his fame or even retired. Yet when HIV, which causes AIDS, was discovered, Salk began work on a vaccine to combat it. He was still working on the vaccine when he died in 1995.

Activity

A CLOSE SECOND Albert Sabin, a medical researcher in Cincinnati, Ohio, was also busy working on a polio vaccine at the same time Salk was developing his. Sabin championed a vaccine with weakened "live" viruses, instead of dead ones. This ran a risk of infecting a person with the very disease it was intended to prevent. As it turned out, although Salk's vaccine was the first to enter into public use, Sabin's contribution was immense too.

What are the ethics of testing a vaccine by giving it to people it could possibly harm? Research the different approaches of Salk and Sabin and, along with some classmates, assume the roles of doctors on a medical board in the 1950s that has to make decisions about following Salk and Sabin's recommendations. Remember, you don't personally have to hold the opinion of the "character" you are role playing.

Ebola Fever

Atlanta, Georgia, 1976—The Centers for Disease Control

Several scientists pass security checks and enter a level 4 lab. This is where the deadliest viruses known are studied. The scientists put on full bodysuits and breathe pumped-in oxygen. They hover over a box containing tissue and blood samples. The box is under a hood that removes the surrounding air so there is absolutely no threat of contamination. These scientists are on a dangerous mission to discover the cause of hundreds of deaths halfway around the globe.

A Remote African Village, 1976

A teacher named Mabalo Lokela arrives with a high fever at a cinder block hospital in a remote village. He's just come back from traveling through the jungles of northern Zaire with his friends. There are many fever-inducing pathogens in that part of the world, but the most likely cause is thought to be malaria. Doctors treat Lokela for malaria and release him to his family. Two days later, he's back. The fever still rages, and he's vomiting blood. The staff treats him with everything from antibiotics to vitamins, but nothing works, and he dies after two weeks of suffering. His wife, mother, and sister prepare his body for the funeral and are struck with fever. They die of the same symptoms. Healthcare workers are also getting sick. The deadly disease is spreading, and no one knows what it is. Surrounding villages are fearful. The cinder block hospital is a place where people are dying horrible deaths. The country's health authorities arrive to see men, women, and children dropping like flies. People are in a state of shock and near panic. Blood and tissue samples are sent to laboratories around the world to identify this killer.

The World Responds

It is under these circumstances that Ebola was revealed. The method of transmission was determined early on to be contact with those infected; but try as they might, doctors could do nothing for people who had already contracted the virus. This virus was swift and deadly. The only hope was to stop it from spreading. Doctors from all over the world had to go to the source and contain it. Dressed in protective suits that covered them from head to toe, an international medical team descended on the village amid abandoned hospitals and many dead bodies. Houses were burned to the ground and sick people were not allowed to leave home until the sickness had passed. The team scoured the villages for new cases, but the epidemic was over. Three hundred people had come down with Ebola, and 280 had died.

Hopeful Signs

Since then, Ebola has popped up every once in a while, but it is essentially gone. Where did it come from? Chances are that the virus had lived undisturbed in the jungles of Africa, infecting monkeys. When humans venture into an infected territory, they can stir up new viruses. When we meet new viruses, our bodies are unprepared, and disease can occur.

Because of scientist-detectives like those at the Centers for Disease Control (CDC), the virus that caused this epidemic is now known to us. Through places like the CDC, scientists can study the virus and learn ways to prevent it from spreading and killing again.

As for a cure, maybe you'll be the one who discovers it.

Are Viruses in Your Future?

Are you into solving mysteries, doing detective work, and dodging danger? Does using top technology to look into the tiny world of mysterious things fascinate you? Then you might make a great microbiologist!

You may be asking yourself, "What's a microbiologist?" It's a scientist who studies living organisms and infectious agents. Microbiologists also study the interaction of these microorganisms and people. So what exactly do microbiologists do and where do they work? Though they are often found huddling and sharing research with other scientists, you can find them in almost every industry imaginable. Among the hands-on jobs available in microbiological science are:

- **Bacteriologist:** Studies how bacteria reproduce and infect humans, animals, and plants.

- **Microbial physiologist and biochemist:** Investigates how and from where organisms get energy and nutrients, how these organisms use energy and nutrients, and how they reproduce or divide themselves.

- **Mycologist:** Studies fungi, molds, and yeasts to discover how they infect living matter, reproduce, and cause disease.

- **Parasitologist:** Works with parasitic organisms to find out how they infect living hosts, reproduce, and cause disease.

- **Virologist:** Concentrates on viruses or pieces of genetic material that are active only inside living cells.

Microbiologists by any name usually try to have many other skills that may help them in their work. In college, you'll find that you can combine a science education with another discipline, such as business, marketing, law, or journalism. This would make it easier for you to find scientific jobs in sales, grant-writing (helping companies find money to fund their projects), public relations, regulatory affairs (for example, making and petitioning for laws or special government projects dealing with research), or management.

It's a Small World

1. North America

In the fall of 1981, deaths from a mysterious disease were reported in Los Angeles and San Francisco. Soon, similar deaths were reported in New York. Although education and preventive measures have helped decrease the rate of new cases, it has by no means been stopped. About half of new cases of HIV are among young people in the 15 to 24 age range.

The world's population is on the go. It's easier than ever to get on a plane and jet to faraway places. It's also easier for viruses to travel. One virus that has definitely earned its frequent-flier miles is HIV, which can cause AIDS. In at least two different forms, it has produced an epidemic, infecting people all over the world. People can get the virus through sexual activity with infected individuals, infected blood transfusions, sharing intravenous needles with infected drug users, and other times their blood mixes with an infected person's blood. A child born to an infected mother may also be infected.

What does HIV do? HIV is short for Human Immunodeficiency Virus, which attacks a person's immune system, preventing it from fighting off disease. AIDS is short for Acquired Immune Deficiency Syndrome. Not everyone infected with HIV develops symptoms of AIDS right away. In some people, they may not show up for years. In others, however, the virus chips away at the immune system, making copies of itself and destroying cells. Strange infections occur. If a person becomes sufficiently weakened, these infections can be fatal, because the immune system is so damaged it can no longer fight. Right now, there are treatments that help some people manage the disease, and scientists are working on vaccines and cures.

2. Caribbean

Appeared in the late 1970s. The rising number of new cases indicates that the epidemic is still growing.

3. Latin America

Appeared in the late 1970s. Most prominent in men. It is also on the rise in women, who now make up 20 percent or more of cases.

4. Western Europe

Began appearing here in the early 1980s. Though the number of cases of HIV has increased, the number of people dying of AIDS has decreased due to anti-HIV drugs.

5. Eastern Europe and Central Asia

Until the early 1990s, this area seemed as if it might be spared the worst of the epidemic. However, now the virus is spreading wildly through populations in these countries, mainly due to drug use and unprotected sex.

8. East Asia and the Pacific

This area has been much less hard hit than the countries to the south.

9. Southeast Asia

Large populations and travel have helped spread the disease.

6. North Africa and the Middle East

The area above the Sahara has been affected far less than Sub-Saharan Africa.

7. Sub-Saharan Africa

Many scientists believe AIDS comes from a virus that might have infected monkeys in Africa. Possibly, humans began to get the disease through animal bites. In Africa, cases of AIDS have been recorded since the 1970s. But people have probably been dying from it for much longer.

10. Australia and New Zealand

The number of new cases is growing, mostly among young people.

Activity

THE SAME YET DIFFERENT You'll need a group of people. Start with a secret sentence. Write it down but don't show it or tell it to anyone. Whisper it to one person. Have that person whisper it to the next and then so on, until it reaches the last person. Have the last person write down what the sentence was. Then take a look at how different the first and the last sentence are. The sentence changed a little with each person that repeats it—kind of like a virus. Viruses such as HIV are quick-change artists—mutating to stay alive. That's how they've survived for so long.

SOUTHWEST

Southwest, United States, 1993

It's been a good year for crops. Plenty of rain. The pine nut harvest is a record high. Everyone in the Navajo nation is well stocked for food. But something is going on.

A twenty-one-year-old Navajo athlete, in excellent condition, collapses. She can't breathe. Her lungs fill up with fluid and she dies. Five days later, her fiancé—also a Navajo athlete in peak condition—dies on the way to her funeral. Her brother and his wife also contract the disease. Reports come in that other healthy Navajo Indians are also dying of sudden respiratory failure. Alarm bells are going off in the Southwest. What's going on?

You decide to investigate. You arrive at the woman's home and look around. Could it be that she was being poisoned? You look for open containers of chemicals. When you open the door, you notice dark pellets everywhere. There is a container of kitchen cleanser opened on the counter. In the pantry, there are sacks of grains, nuts, and dried fruits. The sacks appear to have been gnawed through.

Someone enters the house. It is an old shaman who tells you that this kind of sickness is not new. It has happened before—whenever the rains are plentiful and the pine nut harvests are bountiful.

Scientists struggle to discover what is causing the epidemic. You think you know. What's going on? How can you stop its spread?

PLAGUE

(Answer is on page 32)

Clues

Use these clues . . .

Evidence:

▶ Pellets were everywhere.

▶ Record pine nut harvest.

▶ Bags of grain, nuts, and dried fruit were gnawed open.

▶ Open bottle of kitchen cleanser.

▶ What did the victims have in common? They were Navajos. They were otherwise healthy. They lived in rural areas.

▶ The sickness has happened before when harvests were plentiful.

Activity

HOW WOULD YOU STOP AN OUTBREAK? Write a short story depicting a mysterious outbreak. Where is the setting for the outbreak? How does it spread? What happens to the victims? Then come up with a step-by-step plan to stop your virus from spreading.

THAT'S CATCHY!

The Cold Facts on the Common Cold

There are nearly 61 million cases of the common cold annually. That's a lot of sneezing and wheezing. More than 27 million cases affect Americans under age 17. There are nearly 22 million lost school days annually due to the common cold.

Smallsville

Five thousand cold viruses lined up side by side could stretch across this period.

Even Smaller

So you think viruses are small. How about parts of viruses, such as viral proteins? (See the diagram on page 4 to get an idea of how these compare to viruses.) Another tiny critter is the prion. It may be small, but watch out!

DEADLY DESTROYERS

Prions are tiny protein particles that are capable of transmitting deadly diseases. Unlike viruses, prions have no genetic information that would allow them to duplicate and spread inside other cells. Prions (short for "proteinaceous infectious particle"—a very long name for such a little thing?) do their damage by corrupting another protein that normally exists on the surface of human cells. This causes brain cells to malfunction and die, leading to loss of coordination and dementia in the host.

Here are six prion diseases, all of them fatal:

▶ **Scrapie** (sheep)

▶ **Chronic wasting disease** (deer and elk)

▶ **Feline spongiform encephalopathy** (cats)

▶ **Creutzfeldt-Jacob disease** (humans)

▶ **Fatal familial insomnia** (humans)

▶ **Kuru or "laughing death,"** transmitted by ritual cannibalism (humans)

FOSSIL EVIDENCE SHOWS THAT DINOSAURS BATTLED WITH VIRAL INFECTIONS

The vector-borne group of diseases is made up of organisms that spend part of their life inside a mosquito, flea, tick, or other arthropod, and the other part of their life inside a vertebrate. The arthropod (or "vector") picks up the disease agent when it bites a sick or infected host. It then carries the disease to one or more new hosts during its next blood meals.

Mosquitoes were already feeding on blood during the days of the dinosaurs. We know this because blood-feeding arthropods, such as mosquitoes, fleas, and ticks, were caught in sticky tree sap millions of years ago. The sap later hardened into amber. Many viruses, bacteria, protozoa, worms, and other parasitic organisms have spent millions of years adapting their own life cycles to the intimate relationships between biting arthropods and their hosts.

How Long Has This Been Going On?

Outside a cell, a virus remains dormant—often in a crystallized form—able to survive for years, floating around the air or buried under rock or in the soil. Viruses can remain in this inert state for years, springing to life as soon as they make contact with the right kind of cell.

Infectious HUMOR

What do you get when you cross a comic with a virus?

Sick jokes

How did the virus get from Paris to New York?

It "flu."

What did one virus say to the other who was humming a tune?

That's catchy

Stop, You Demon!

A common belief long ago was that right after a sneeze, demons rushed in through your nose and mouth. So people developed the habit of covering their mouth and nose when they sneezed—not out of politeness or cleanliness, but out of fear of losing their souls. They had no idea this practice helped stop the spread of viruses that were the cause of colds.

Egypt, 1156 B.C.

Mummy Isn't Feeling Well

King Ramses V dies mysteriously. Three thousand years later, his mummified body is dug up and unwrapped. His body shows signs of terrible pockmarked scars, which suggests he may have died of smallpox. Other mummies had shrunken arms and legs—telltale signs of polio.

Europe, the Middle Ages

GOOD HEAVENS The

flu, more formally known as influenza, was so named because people believed it was caused by the influence of the stars. The tiny microbes were not yet known about, and people in those days believed the patterns of the heavens were responsible for other aspects of life—so why not illness?

Final Project:
Designer Viruses

Viruses can be both horrible and fascinating. Based on what you know about viruses, design a virus of your own. Think through your creation from as many angles as possible, write detailed descriptions, and make drawings to accompany them.

❶ What is the purpose of your virus?

❷ What does the target host cell look like? This will be important before you determine what your virus looks like. For example, if the cell has tiny hooks, your virus will need a way to attach.

❸ What does the virus look like?

❹ How will the virus enter the host, replicate, and do what it is meant to do?

❺ What are the effects of using the virus? How might it affect the food web, the ecosystem?

❻ How might the virus affect your life? Should you think twice about unleashing it on the world?

ANSWERS

Solve-It-Yourself Mystery, pages 28–29: The disease was a virus spread by mice. Those tiny pellets were their droppings.

You can rule out poison because there were other forms of life in the house—mice, rats, and the medicine man. Kitchen cleaners will not kill a person if they are just opened on the counter. If she drank the kitchen cleaner, she would have been the only one to die—obviously the disease was something that could spread—like a virus. If the medicine man told of previous instances occurring when harvests were bountiful, then it is possible that the disease was spread through the mice that were also plentiful when the food was plentiful.

The disease was a virus spread though the feces of mice. People that came in contact with the mice could contact the disease. If the Navajo population experienced a large harvest then the whole nation shared in the goods. Plentiful goods means more mice. Get rid of the mice, get rid of the danger.